Vegetables

Vintage Pictures and advertising

Retro Books

Presentation

This book consists of a non-systematic series of images to collect, see, and, above all, to use for decoration purposes.

It was designed so that you can detach all images or each one individually, allowing you to frame the pictures you like the most.

The purpose of this book is aesthetic only, to assemble together beautiful images which take us to charming places in the history of great brands of food and drinking products. It is a tribute to so many advertisement creators and label designers that will forever remain in our memories.

For this reason, we do not indicate dates or researches that we made throughout the process of making this book.

Retro Books

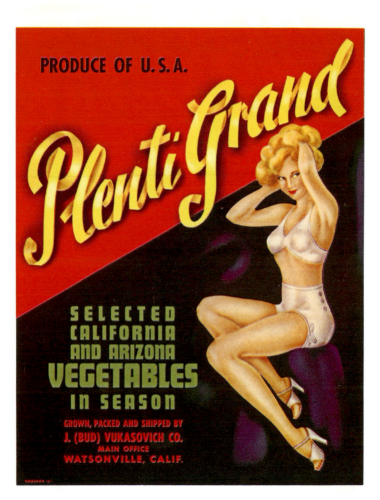

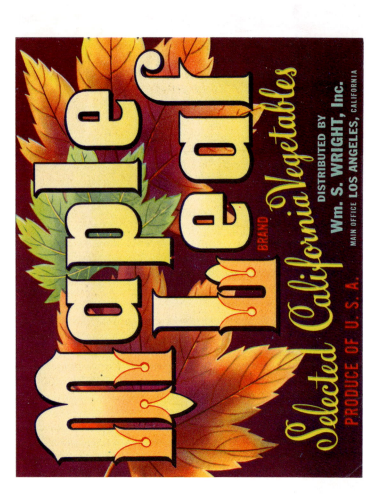

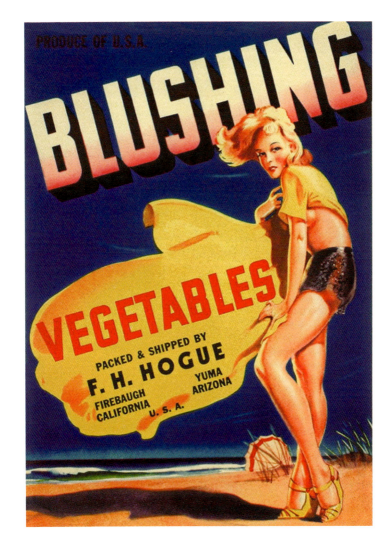

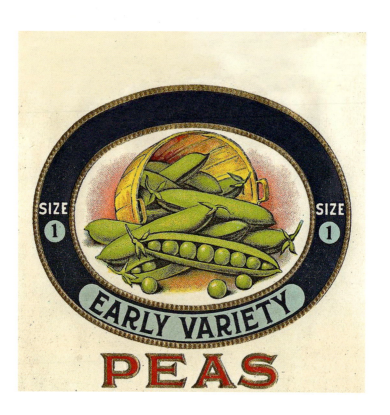

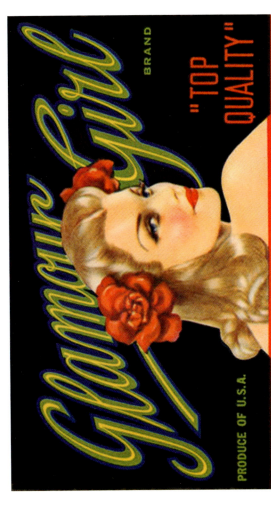

MARY AGNES
BRAND
U.S. No. 1
Louisiana
SWEET POTATOES
PORTO RICAN
Yams
HAND SELECTED
HAND PACKED
50 LBS. NET
PRODUCE OF U.S.A.

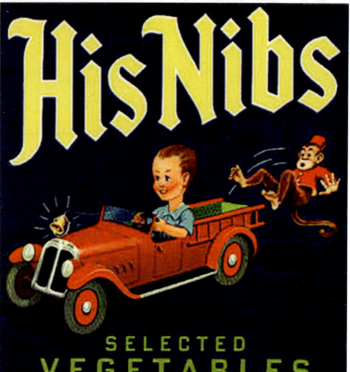

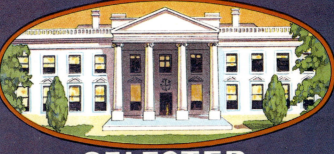

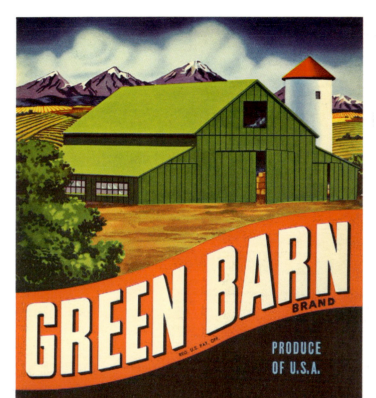

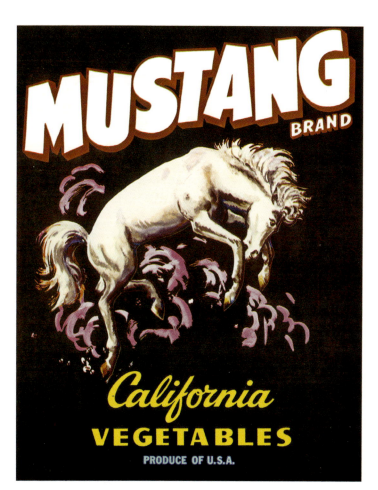

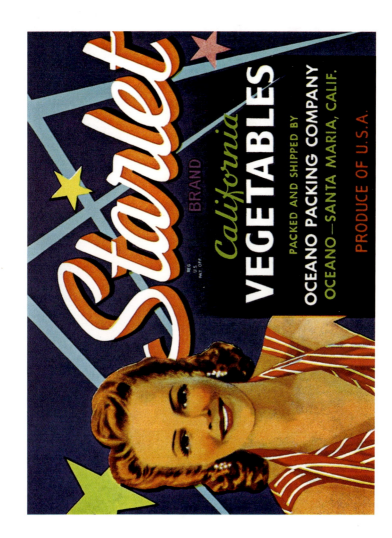

KREME de KOKE

BRAND

SELECTED
VEGETABLES

SALINAS GROWERS EXCHANGE

GROWERS SHIPPERS

SALINAS · CALIFORNIA

PRODUCE OF U.S.A.

PRODUCE OF U.S.A.

FOOT HIGH

VEGETABLES

PACKED AND SHIPPED BY

F. H. HOGUE

FIREBAUGH, CALIFORNIA—YUMA, ARIZONA., U.S.A.

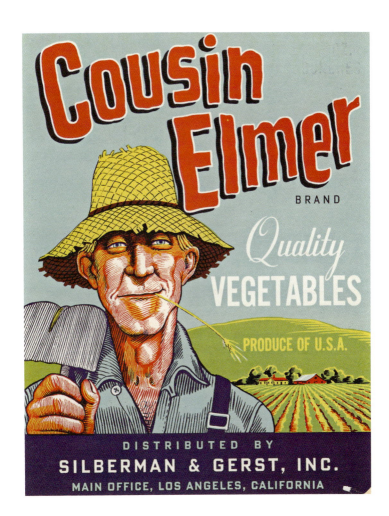

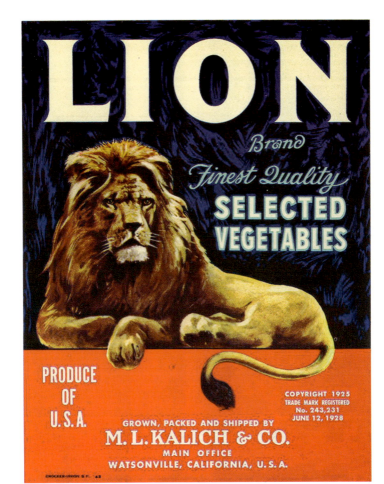

ELKHORN

BRAND

SELECTED
GREEN PEAS

ELKHORN FRUIT CO., LODI
LEONARDINI . . . MAGGIO
GROWERS PACKERS SHIPPERS
MAIN OFFICE:
LODI, CALIFORNIA

PRODUCE

F C
E
OF U.S.A.

ELKHORN FRUIT CO., LODI

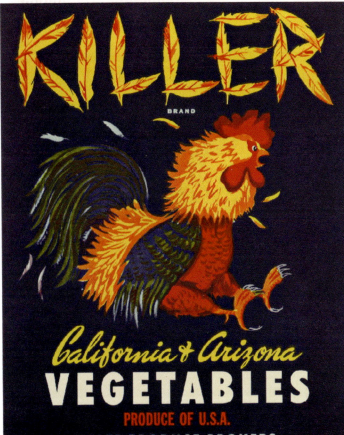

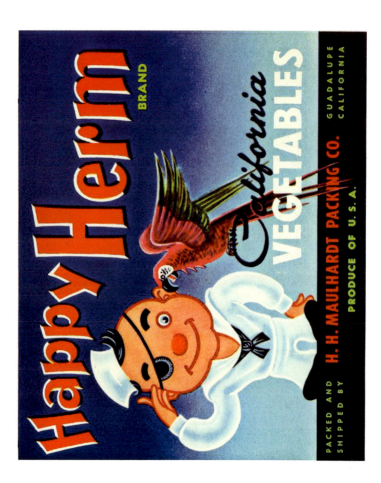

PEP

BRAND

PRODUCE OF U.S.A.

SELECT

VEGETABLES

DISTRIBUTED BY

NASH-DE CAMP COMPANY

VISALIA CALIFORNIA

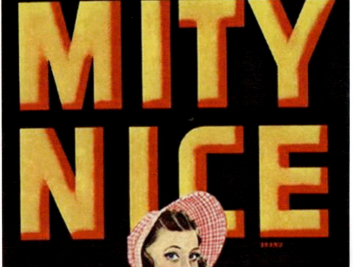

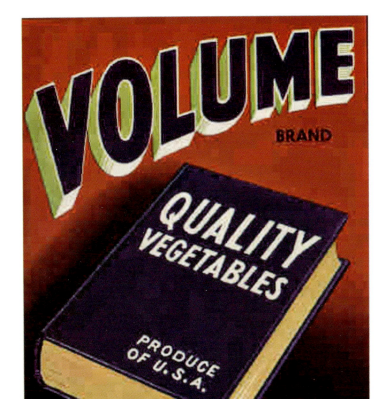

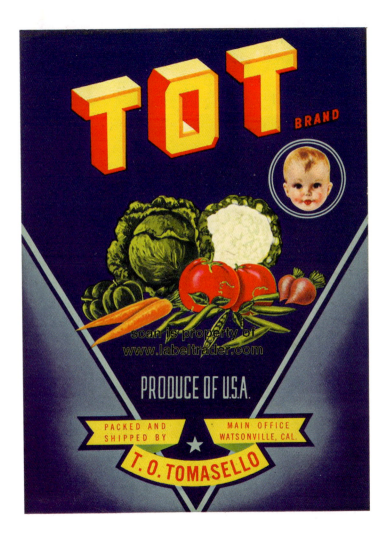

"Sweet Patootie"
BRAND
Selected
VEGETABLES
DISTRIBUTED BY
KAVANAGH DISTRIBUTING CO.
LOS ANGELES, CALIF.
PRODUCE OF U.S.A.
T. M. REG. U. S. PAT. OFF.
scan is property of

Snow Slide

BRAND

CALIFORNIA VEGETABLES

PACKED BY MONTEREY BAY PACKING CO., CASTROVILLE, CALIF.

PRODUCE OF U.S.A.

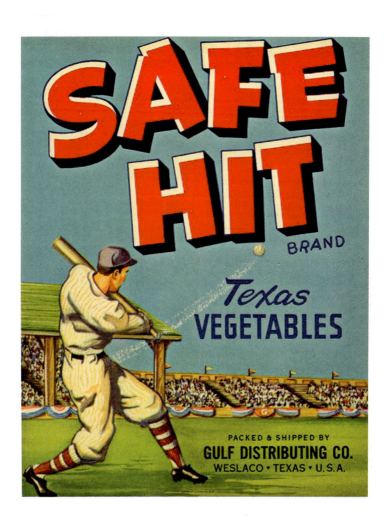

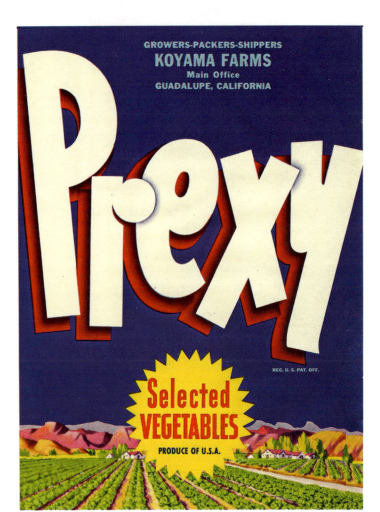

PRODUCE OF U.S.A.
COCKSURE
BRAND
California
Fruits and Vegetables
DISTRIBUTED BY
COCHRAN CO., INC.
MAIN OFFICE TRACY • CALIFORNIA

GAY JOHNNY

Texas
VEGETABLES

PRODUCE OF U.S.A.

PACKED & SHIPPED BY J. S. McMANUS PRODUCE CO. WESLACO, TEXAS

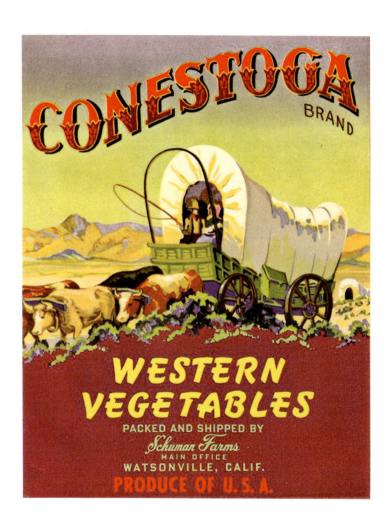

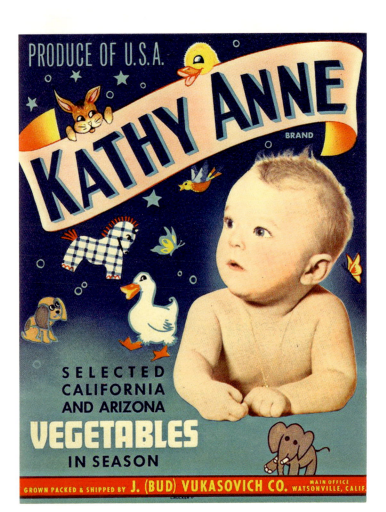

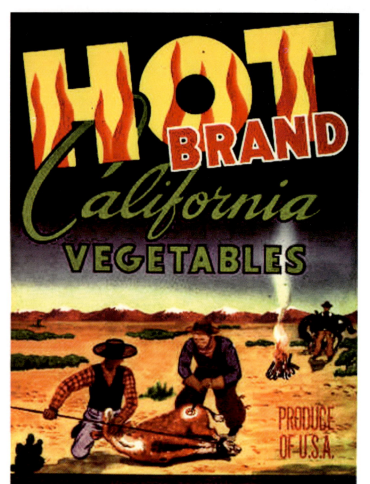

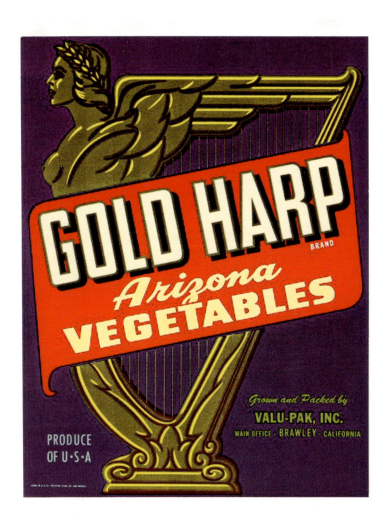

GARDEN GATE

"GATEWAY TO THE VALLEY OF GREEN GOLD"

Selected

VEGETABLES

PACKED AND SHIPPED BY

SALINAS MARKETING COOPERATIVE

SALINAS, CALIFORNIA

PRODUCE OF U.S.A.

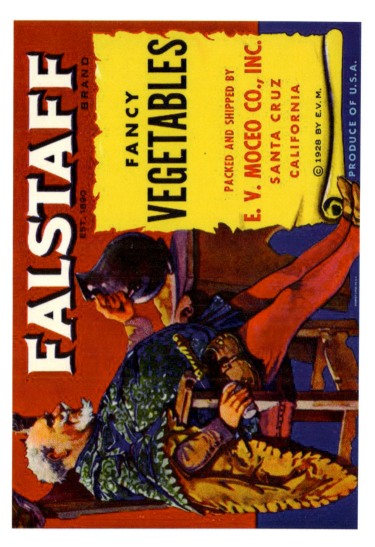

Unit 16 & 17. 12F, Tower A
New Mandarim Plaza,14
Science Museum Rd. TST East
Kowloon, Hong Kong

Printed in Chine